Written By
P.E. Barnes

Illustrators:
F. Nerob & R. Rojone

D1410297

Dedication

I dedicate this book to all the girls in the world

that dare to dream of building a real-estate

empire.

Riley owns one of the largest real-estate portfolios

held by any woman in America.

Riley's passion for real-estate investing began while

working as a real-estate agent. A real-estate agent

helps people buy and sell real estate.

Riley helps buyers obtain a mortgage to buy a

house. A mortgage, is a loan used to finance a

property.

Riley began working with real-estate investors that buy properties to acquire wealth and improve neighborhoods through rehabbing. She was inspired by the difference they were making in communities and the profits they received from investing in real estate.

Riley decided to purchase a fixer-upper home to flip into a beautiful home for a nice family. One of her clients became a mentor to ensure her first flip was successful.

After hiring contractors to fix up the home, Riley

sold the home to a nice family. She made a good

profit from the sale of her first flip.

Riley was so thrilled with her first house flipping project

that she decided to buy a small apartment building. She was

able to earn passive income on a monthly basis.

Riley set her goals high and began to partner with other investors, and she flipped 50 single family homes per year. She used her profits from flipping to buy large apartment buildings, hotels, and retail malls.

Riley became one of the country's most famous real-estate agents and mogul. She met a man named Robert, who was also a real-estate mogul. They married and had a beautiful family.

Riley was an inspiration to many girls and women across the world. She employed thousands of people through her real-estate company, from the contractors to the people that worked in the hotels.

Riley retired as a billionaire and was very proud of her success and helping others. Her children worked in the family business. Riley and Robert created generational wealth for their family.

The
End

Vocabulary Words

Fixer upper- a house in need of repair.

Real estate- property consisting of land or buildings.

Real estate portfolio- a collection of properties that are held and managed to achieve a financial goal.

Passive income- is money you earn in a way that requires little to no daily effort to maintain.

Real-estate Investor- a person that buys real estate to generate income.

Profits- a financial gain; the difference between the amount earned and the amount spent in buying, operating, or producing something.

Flipping- buying an undervalued property and reselling it for a profit within a few months or up to a year.

Rehab- restoring a property through repairs and upgrades.

Real Estate Goals

About the Author

P.E. Barnes is a real estate investor in Chicago. She is passionate about educating children about financial literacy. She is a wife and mother of two young boys that inspired this book series.

For bookings or inquiries email: littleowners@gmail.com

Made in the USA
Middletown, DE
14 June 2022

67135928R00018